Children Die, Too

For parents who are experiencing the death of a child

By Joy and Dr. S.M. Johnson, Centering Corporation

Illustrations by Caroline Crider, San Antonio, TX

Layout by Janet Sieff, Centering Corporation

Additional copies may be ordered from:
Centering Corporation
PO Box 4600
Omaha, NE 68104

Phone: 402-553-1200
Fax: 402-553-0507
e-mail: j1200@aol.com
Website: www.centering.org

D0113545

Dedicated to the memory of Linda, who died at age 3. One of us parented her and loved her while she lived, and the other has come to love her through a shared memory.

In Loving Memory of:

Born:

Died:

That which we lose we mourn, but we must rejoice that we have ever had.

C.J. Wells

I Remember, I Remember

By Joy Johnson, Centering Corporation

In the Spring, when the first crocus pokes its head tentatively out of the frozen ground, I think of you and I remember, I remember.

In the Summer, when the blaring heat wilts the rose petals and paints unsightly cracks in the ground, I think of you and I remember, I remember.

In the Autumn, when the trees are ablaze in the glory of fall and my shoes make crackling sounds as I walk, I think of you and I remember, I remember.

And in the winter, when I sit at my window to watch a blizzard whirl snow around my grief and loneliness, then, too, I think of you and I remember, yes, I remember.

A Note from Joy and Marv

In the Mormon Cemetery in Omaha, Nebraska, there is an awesome statue. Two pioneer parents stand over the open grave of their child, their heads close together -- the winter wind blowing their capes as the father's hand holds his shovel. It is an extremely touching artwork.

The cemetery itself is filled with the graves of children who died during the Mormon encampment. In that time, when our great grandparents were raising families, the death of children was common. It was not unusual to bury one child or perhaps more, and the family who did **not** lose a child was rare.

Fewer children die now. We are a society which readily accepts the death of the aged. We will even tolerate the death of adults. It is extremely hard for us to admit that children die, too.

Living after the death of a child is not done according to a fixed pattern of emotions. The various feelings and experiences are more like changes in weather. About the time you believe the storm has passed, you find it returning to stir you again. Some parents have described their grief as coming in waves. Just when you least expect it, you are struck by the wave and carried along with it. Grief is something you integrate into your life. You don't "get through it" or "get over it." You make it a part of you, just as your child will always be a part of you and never forgotten.

Children Die, Too shares these many feelings that come with the death of a child.

Shock

Everyone knows children get sick.

Everyone knows children get hurt.

Everyone knows children can die.

Everyone knows, but not really.

Not me! Not mine! Not now!

It is hard to believe your child is dead. The feeling of dullness that comes when you know your child is dying or that your child is dead is a form of shock. It is your mind's way of protecting you and allowing in only the amount of pain that you can handle at the time. It is a normal, healthy response. When you are ready, the shock will fade.

It is like living in a fog or a cloud. It is like being encased in soft plastic. It is a time when decisions are difficult.

You may find yourself forgetting things you've already decided upon. You may start out on one errand and find yourself in an entirely different store. You may find yourself standing for five full minutes trying to decide between the can of peas and the can of beans. This is a time of confusion that interferes with your decision-making. Allow yourself some time on any major decisions you need to make. This is also a time to check out your important decisions with someone who can help you see more clearly. It may be helpful to make a list of what you need to get done. Mark them off as they are completed. It may also help to start a journal of daily events. You can also write about your feelings, questions and answers, and about the changes taking place. Writing can be a big help in working through your grief.

Shock will diminish. It will come and go along with other feelings, such as anger.

Anger

Of all the feelings that come when your child dies, anger is sometimes the most difficult to accept. You may have been taught that anger is bad, or that only men are allowed to be angry, or that it is wrong to be angry at God.

I'm so angry! And there's nowhere to put it. I don't feel right being angry at the lady who ran over Karen. She was anguished about it. I don't feel right being mad at Karen for stepping off the curb at the wrong time or her father for not being with her, but somewhere inside I am angry, even at God.

Mother in Des Moines

Your child's death is an extremely anger-provoking experience. Anger seems to be all around you, with nowhere to direct it. Parents may blame each other and snap at the kids.

Children act out the anger in fights. Doctors become cold. Nurses get snippy. Ministers may try to explain it away. Many people deny their feelings and become guilty about being angry.

It's all right to feel angry about your child's death. The first agonized "why" after your child dies is often an expression of anger. Learning to share your anger appropriately can bring a real release of pressure from within. It may even help you avoid extended depression.

When you feel angry you may want to try exercising: take a brisk walk, jog, swim, do something physical that harms no one, not even yourself. Talk about your anger with someone you trust. Some parents have found that hitting a bed with a kitchen towel brings relief, and others have just gone somewhere safe and quiet and screamed.

As you learn to express yourself, you may come to realize that God can handle your anger, too. If you think it's wrong to state anger toward God, just read the Prophets. They were often angry at God, revealed that anger, and found their relationship with God to be rich and full.

Another feeling mixed in with shock and anger is sadness.

Sadness

When your child dies, you cry! Sometimes when people cry they say they "break down." Actually, crying is more like a gentle melting, a warm experience.

You may hold back tears because you're afraid that if you start crying you'll never be able to stop. You will, when you and your body are ready.

You may feel embarrassed to cry in front of people, or you may be concerned about their discomfort. It's not only all right to cry in front of people, it is also very acceptable to cry with them. Remember, it's not your job to take care of other people right now.

After the death of your child, there will be days when getting up doesn't feel worth the effort. You experience depression.

Depression

When your child dies, you feel the slow emptiness of loss. You tend to move more slowly through your depression as your mind absorbs your loss. During depression you may feel like giving up, not wanting to live. You may have a sense of meaninglessness and a need for release.

It's not unnatural to have thoughts of suicide or fears of going crazy. It can be a frightening time. At such times it may help you to look honestly at your feelings and your fears. Some parents have set aside a certain amount of time just for crying.

I had half an hour in the morning and the same amount of time in the afternoon that was totally devoted to tears. After that time I made myself get up and do something. At work I cried in the bathroom.
                                                            Mother in Omaha

It may help to talk with a supportive person about your feelings. Choose someone who will listen without telling you what you should or should not feel. Check with your clergy person or hospital staff about support groups in your area.

Another feeling may be an overwhelming sense of guilt.

Guilt

> *If only.*
> *If only.*
> *If only.*

You will hear yourself using these words. Most parents whose child has died have periods when they feel guilty. A part of the guilt is wanting to undo what was done. . . to stop time, to redo a day or minute that might have made a difference.

Our culture teaches people to be hard on themselves and blame themselves when anything goes wrong. Because of this, we tend to feel responsible when children die, too.

If only I had kept him in longer. If only I had been there. If only I had known. If only! If only! If only!

We are people who want answers. It goes against all our beliefs, hopes, and dreams when children die. You will search and look for answers to questions which sometimes have no answers.

Blaming yourself is one way of attaching some kind of meaning to a situation which makes no sense, of trying to answer the unanswerable why questions. When you feel guilty, recognize it for what it is. . .a searching for an answer. If you could have prevented your child's death, you would have. You and your family are not to blame.

No matter what you do to work through your grief, you'll find that everyone has different feelings and emotions.

Everyone Has Feelings

Most people looking in from the outside think a child's death makes you closer. Actually, the opposite is often true.

You may want to blame your partner. Everything you have fought about, disagreed over, disliked in each other may come out again as you live through this intense time.

You may lash out at your partner. You may turn your partner into a mind-reader by assuming your feelings are just naturally known, even when you don't share them.

You may resent your partner for not sharing feelings. Talk about how you can help each other.

Both you and your partner will grieve differently and in your own ways.

Recognize and talk about your and your partner's strengths. Talk about the good times you've shared together. Take an evening out once a week, or even take a vacation together. Ask for what you need. Say what will help you. Give as best you can when you are asked by your partner. Remember that your primary relationship is to your partner, not to your child, your child's memory, or your grief. Get to know each other all over again.

Having a child die can batter your own self-esteem. You may feel you have failed your child, let her down, not been there when you were needed. All this can pour over into your relationship. You can feel you are a failure as a parent, too. These feelings are very real, even if they aren't true.

Remember, each of you will grieve differently, but each of you will grieve. When you begin to accept your differences you can begin to help each other heal. When one is up, the other may be down. Allow each other space and time. Talk about how you met and how you came to fall in love.

Grandparents

People not only tend to think relationships become closer after a child dies, they also have an image of the loyal, helpful family gathering together. This is not always true either.

If your child was ill for a long time, you are probably aware that your extended family had some struggle and difficulty. They may even have posed some problems for you when you were counting on them for support.

Grandparents have a two-part grief. They have lost a grandchild. They may also feel they have lost you.

Your parents may feel a tremendous inadequacy in their own ability to help you. You are no longer the little child coming to them for help and comfort. They may wish to take you on their laps and rock you. They want you to feel better, to be all right again. They don't always know how to support you now. You may need to guide them.

You may find yourself, time and again, chief comforter of those who come to comfort you. This can be true not only of your parents, but also of your friends.

I can't buy her an even better child like I used to buy her a better doll when one broke. I can't tell her she'll get over it like I did when a boyfriend dumped her. I can't hold her and rock her and tuck her into bed and tell her it will all be all right in the morning. It won't. I can't take her hand and sit her down and give her instructions on how to do this grief thing. I can listen to her and I can dry her cheeks and I can hold her and hug her and talk to her, and I can recognize that her loss is much greater than mine. And maybe, on some of the worst days, we can be two women who walk to the corner and have an ice cream cone and cry together.

Grandmother in Maine

If you have other children, know that they are grieving, too.

Your Other Children

You and your partner knew life without your child that died. The child's brothers and sisters may not have. Death can be very frightening and confusing for the children. They are just learning how to grieve.

They may have fears of becoming sick and dying, too.

They may fear separation.

They may be afraid to ask questions because it will upset you.

They may question your love.

Children need to be treated with respect and dignity. Give them straight and honest answers. Allow them to express their feelings. Tell them you love them. Tell them it's okay for all of you to cry. Let them know you're glad they are alive. This can help children work through their grief, a grief which may show up in different ways.

When children grieve you're likely to see a lot of behaviors. Children may have temper tantrums, revert back to bedwetting and finger sucking. They may be more withdrawn or more aggressive. Nightmares are common. Many will experience some health problems.

This is a time when children need to understand that while you will all be sad for a long time, things will get better.

Toddlers and preschoolers will tend to fear being abandoned. They will be afraid and want you with them more. Children between five and nine years of age see death as a ghost or angel and that it happens to other things and other people. Having death happen to another child can be very upsetting.

Even while they are grieving, children will take time out for play and have times of great normalcy.

Teens will grieve in their own way. They may want to spend even more time with friends.

I just wanted someone to come by and take me out for pizza. The whole house was so sad and dark. I needed to get out.

Teen in San Francisco

Children of all ages are likely to experience some feelings of guilt. Young children think magically. They may really believe their thoughts or wishing killed their sibling. They need to be told very firmly that they are not to blame.

And they may feel responsible. Every child wishes a sister or brother wasn't around at times. On occasion, kids wish their brothers and sisters dead. They need to be told that these kinds of thoughts do not cause death.

Dear Parents,

My sister, Deanne was in a tragic car accident in May. A week later, on Mother's Day, Deanne died a brain death. When Deanne died, it felt like I died, too! What I find helps me cope is:

Talking to my Mom and Dad.
Writing down how I feel.
Crying as much as I want.

My dog and cat seem to help me cope with some bad days. I can tell my animals anything and everything I feel, and I know they will always keep it private! There isn't a replacement for Deanne, but it is always nice to have my animals and family.

When I first found out that Deanne had died, I couldn't think of any reason why life should go on. But I realize now that time does not stand still; although it took me a year and a half to realize it. Time can be your worst enemy or it can be your best friend. It's what you make of it that counts.

Time is still the age-old medicine. It heals in measured doses, slowly, surely.

DENISE CARLSON'S SISTER DIED AT AGE 16.
FROM THE BOOK, **DEAR PARENTS**, © CENTERING CORPORATION, 1989.

Age Appropriate Responses

Each child, like each adult, grieves differently and according to their own personality. However, children do experience behavioral stages, where some grief reactions may be common. Knowing these stages occur can help us support and care for the children.

Infants	More crying Thumb or finger sucking Senses anxiety, sorrow
1-2 Years	May cling Doesn't want parent to leave May sleep more May wake frequently May be more "hyper"
3-5 Years	Bedwetting is common Unable to verbalize feelings May ask questions 'Plays "death" Reverts to baby talk May want bottle and diapers
6-10 Years	Plays "death" and "funeral" Shyness may increase Acting out may increase Grades may suffer School may become safe haven
11-Teens	Anger is normal Feelings that life is "unfair" Acting out occurs Philosophical talk with friends Search for Spirituality Risky behaviors not uncommon

What You Can Do

Infants	Keep to baby's schedule Keep baby in her own home with few visitors Talk to infant as you hold him
1-2 Years	Be honest Answer questions Explain what death is Explain some feelings they may have Remind them they did not cause the death Involve them in the funeral Let them know they will be taken care of
3-5 Years	Answer questions Be honest Explain feelings Talk about fears Involve the child in the funeral
6-10 Years	Be honest Answer questions Explain feelings Provide a journal Offer love, understanding and support Involve them in the funeral service
11-Teens	Talk openly about feelings Encourage teens to talk to a school counselor Encourage them to journal or draw Create rituals of memory Tell them what you need Let them tell you what they need

Friends

For friends and society in general, the death of a child is the most difficult to handle. Sara and her husband drove across the state to bury their teenage son who had completed suicide. At home they were community leaders surrounded by caring groups, churches, and social organizations.

One week after her son died, Sara took her five year-old to a school play practice. When she walked into the school, some thirty mothers and children were working on costumes. They looked up at Sara and instead of moving to her, nervously became busy with their work. "Oh well," she sighed. "One of our friends told us we would have to approach people." She walked toward the women at the nearest table, opened up her arms and welcomed the flood of hugs and tears.

Most friends are available for your child's funeral, even through they may not know exactly how to help. Other friends will disappear and not be seen again. New friends, many of whom have also lost children, will appear.

Some of the most difficult times may come for you about three weeks after the funeral when you sit around and ask, "Where is everybody?" The casseroles have all been eaten, the flowers have long ago wilted, and the last thank you card has been mailed.

One young mother found a way to reach friends. After two months of very little personal contact she went to the phone and called every friend she could think of. "You can talk to me just like you used to" she said. The relief from the other end of the line was overwhelming in her friends' need to talk to her, too.

> I can't say anything that will make things better,
>
> but I can be there with you and share the anger,
>
> the pain, the bewilderment.
>
> Most of all, I can let you know that I care
>
> and that I won't abandon you.
>
> Dr. Ruth Hitchcock

16

The following letter is from the book, ***Dear Parents,*** ©Centering Corporation. It is written by Elaine Stillwell. Her two oldest children died in a car accident.

Dear Parents,

When the excruciating pain goes down to your toes and your heart feels like it is in a vise, what do you do? How do you get up in the morning? My heart broke when my beautiful 19 year old daughter, Peggy, was killed instantly in a freak car accident. Four days later, the day after we buried her, her brother Denis, my first-born, died from the same accident, and we had two funerals in one week.

When the last care-giver left our home the evening of Denis' funeral, my husband and I looked at each other and wondered how we, and our remaining child, would survive. We didn't have a clue and had no idea of the long road ahead of us as we attempted to reweave our family tapestry.

As I faced the heartbreaking chore of sorting out my children's possessions while shedding many tears, it upset me to toss out their college I.D. cards, social security cards, library and credit cards, and drivers licenses. It dawned on me how easily they might become erased from the memories of friends and loved ones. I didn't want them erased! I vowed that would never happen. I guess you could say I started a crusade. That became a primary motivating factor for me. That idea got me out of bed in the morning/mourning. I was on fire to tell the world about my children, even though I had limited energy and no definite plan how to do it. I talked about them to everybody, whether I was on the grocery line, bank queue, airplane, or sitting in a doctor's office. Now, people who never met Peggy and Denis tell me that they feel they know them. Do you know what that does for my heart?

On days when I was tempted to stay in bed and pull the covers over my head, trying to run away from my pain, I wondered what my children would think of that. Not much, I figured. How I wanted them to continue to be proud of me, rather than embarrassed, every time they looked down on me from above! I wanted them to smile big grins, pop their buttons, and exclaim, "That's my mom!" That vision fueled me to keep going. I kept praying to Peggy and Denis to give me strength on my journey, and they never let me down. We were a team for survival!

Then, I realized that I did not want to waste this wonderful love I have for my Peggy and Denis. By sharing this special love with others, by reinvesting it, I could keep Peggy's and Denis' memories alive while helping others. In that expression of love, I was really blossoming, too, for I found helping is healing.

I think my crusade has been successful! My children are dearly remembered, and I enjoy the bonus of a meaningful life. Look into your hearts, dear parents, and find your motivating factors.

Single Parents and Step-Parents

Our society is increasing its number of single-parent and stepparent families. Families such as yours are a typical family in today's culture.

There are no basic differences in the intensities of feelings for parents, whether you are married, single, or a stepparent. There is perhaps an unfortunate message of guilt sometimes given to divorced and single parents. It may seem that you've had more than your share of grief, particularly if you have experienced the death of a spouse or marital separation.

All of the old grief may surface again, and you will find yourself working through feelings that you believed were finished and resolved long ago.

Your feelings of past events and griefs can usually be recognized as separate from the ones that arise now, with the death of your child. Your feelings are real and valuable.

It is a hole,
A vacantness.
A scary hollow shell that I find myself in.
Death. The robber. The thief of certainty. The stealer of dreams.
My mind holds a thousand facts, yet there is no answer.
My child died, and, in many ways, so have I.
The Me I knew has vanished and in its place stands
a hollow mold that must be re-filled.

SANDY PRIEBE

Taking Care of Yourself

Physical needs: People who are grieving usually don't drink enough water. Pour some water into a pitcher and know you will drink that entire pitcher during the day. Eat very carefully, take an multiple vitamin and cut out alcohol and smoking. Walk. Exercise. Picture all your excuses not to exercise, then picture yourself releasing them, one by one. Even if you have to force yourself to move, you'll feel better afterward. Avoid drugs if at all possible. Even if you can't sleep, you can rest. Not sleeping usually means you're thinking about and processing your grief, and you need to do that. Catch a nap when you can. Remember - - your child would want the best for you. Do all you can to keep from getting sick.

Emotional needs: Most parents have found that attending even one meeting of a parent support group helps. People there really do know how you feel because they too, have lost a child. Talk to people. Share your feelings. Go easy on yourself. Don't force yourself to concentrate when you can't. Ask for hugs.

Spiritual needs: This can easily be a time of questions and quarrels with God. Allow yourself time to find your way. No one expects you to forget your child. That child will be in your heart forever.

Soon you'll find yourself taking better care of yourself. You'll be concerned again about your appearance, your health, your job. Everyday chores around the house will come easier again, and you'll find yourself laughing. The black cloud will slowly fade, and you'll once again see the beauty in the world.

Grief feels like a cave, an aimless groping into a black, deepening void.
Into your hand I press the only candle I have, a message to flicker in the darkness of your soul:
Grief feels like a cave, but it is not a cave.
Grief is a tunnel, a journey.
The blackness is the same.
The only difference is Hope.

MARILYN GRYTE

Making Sense of it All

We have just begun to talk about some of the feelings and relationships that have come to you and others when your child dies.

You have learned that there are no correct answers and no well drawn roadmaps to guide you through your grief. You have learned that just when you think you are on top of the mountain and everything is going smoothly you find yourself in the valley again.

We hope you will allow yourself time. Recognize and welcome a future which will bring growth and changes. Know that months from now you will feel different and that even in those months there will be times without intense grief.

We hope you will be aware of your feelings, accept them, recognize them and do them honor. Most importantly we hope you honor your child by taking care of yourself.

A Time of Searching

The death of a child often sends you searching.
> For a religion which may bring you comfort and answers.
> For new beliefs to enrich the religion with which you began.
> For growing relationships with your partner, family and friends.
> Searching to find yourself in the midst of it all.

People all around you reach out now with awkwardness, confusion and discomfort. We hope you will accept from them that which you can use and recognize that which you cannot use as gifts offered in good faith. We hope you will find some real people who will challenge you and urge you to move through your grief to a new beauty of life.

A friend whose daughter died received a message which read, *We love our children more tonight because of you.* The death of a child is not a good experience. But in the midst of all the sadness, it can be a very rich one.

This book is intended as a beginning. . .

At unusual times,

in unexpected places:

the supermarket, the ball game,

on the way home from work,

my eyes sting and my throat gets tight.

And then I know

that all I want

is you.

DOROTHY FERGUSON

Caring Organizations

The Compassionate Friends
PO Box 3696
Oak Brook IL 60522
Phone: 877-969-0010
www.compassionatefriends.org

National SHARE Office
St. Joseph Health Center
300 First Capitol Dr
St. Charles MO 63301
Phone: 800-821-6819
www.nationalshareoffice.com

Mothers Against Drunk Drivers
511 E John Carpenter Frwy
Ste 700
Irving TX 75062
Phone: 214-744-6233

In Loving Memory
For loss of your only child.
1416 Green Run Lane
Reston VA 22090
Phone: 703-435-0608

Bereaved Parents USA
PO BOX 410350
St. Louis MO 63141
Phone: 314-878-0890

Bereavement Magazine
5125 N Union Blvd, Ste 4
Colorado Springs, CO 80918
Phone: 800-604-4673

SAVE/Suicide
Phone: 888-511-SAVE
www.save.org

Grief Digest Magazine
PO Box 4600
Omaha, NE 68104
Phone: 402-553-1200
www.griefdigest.com

GriefWatch
2116 NE 18th Ave
Portland, OR 97212
Phone: 503-284-7426
www.griefwatch.com

Grief Inc
9016 Taylorsville Rd, #181
Louisville, KY 40299
Phone: 502-671-0535
www.griefinc.com

In-Sight Books
Helping People Help People
Phone: 800-658-9262
www.insightbooks.com

American Assoc of Suicidology
2459 South Ash St
Denver, CO 80222
Phone: 303-692-0985
www.suicidology.org

www.webhealing.com
Many resources on this page including excerpts from Tom Golden's book ***Swallowed by a Snake:*** *The Gift of the Masculine Side of Healing*

Call Centering Corporation for a free catalog of grief resources.
Phone: 402-553-1200

Other Supportive Resources

For Parents

Goodbye My Child - a handbook for parents; full of information

Later Courtney - a mother says goodbye after the death of her daughter

Remember Lee - a journal after the death of a teen in an accident

For Better Or Worse - keeping a marriage together

Love and Remembrance - a journal for bereaved parents

Never Too Old For a Lullaby - for the death of an adult child

Dear Parents - letters to bereaved parents from bereaved parents

Suicide of a Child - for parents whose child completes suicide

When Winter Follows Spring - for death of an adult child

For Siblings

Lost and Found - Remembering a sister who died from Cancer

Since My Brother Died - English and Spanish

Anna's Scrapbook - a story and journal for ages 8-12

For Grandparents

For Bereaved Grandparents - addresses the double grief of grandparents

For a free grief resource catalog, contact:
Centering Corporation
Phone: 402-553-1200
Online catalog: www.centering.org
E-mail: centeringcorp@aol.com